Bygone
Grimsby

Welcome to Bygone Grimsby where we invite you to step back in time and place at the turn of a page. This book is drawn together from articles and pictures that have previously appeared in our popular Bygones magazine and many new photographs from our Grimsby Telegraph archives.

This book is loosely divided into sections: Around Grimsby, Down the Docks, Gone Fishin', Cleethorpes, Out & About, Sports & Leisure, and When Duty Calls. The pictures, to a certain extent, will take you on a tour round Grimsby, though it hasn't always been possible to follow any strict sequencing.

We should like to take this opportunity of thanking all our marvellous readers who over the years have contributed words and pictures and in doing so helped make the series a success. Many thanks to: Ann Hammond (nee Roberts), Cecilia Roberts, Vernon Godwin, Mrs J Ballard, Tony Short, Norman William Stones, Eve Wivell, Shawn Cottingham, and last but by no means least Lynda Hammond. Please forgive any omissions.

Bygone Grimsby

Contents

Around Grimsby

Preparing to make a delivery on his motorcycle
Mr J.H. Hardy, of Hardy's Superior Ices, poses for the
camera outside the Hamilton Street works.

The Corporation Road terminus to Immingham, taken in about 1925.
Also pictured in the background is Marshall's Victoria Mill and clocktower.

Sailors from HMS Panther team up with a group of French matelots, for a run ashore in Grimsby.
The picture was taken in 1912 on the old Corporation Road Bridge. The central market is in the background and Marshall's Mill at extreme left.

The Prince of Wales (later Edward VIII) officially opened the new
Corporation Road Bridge on 19 July 1928.

The Escart Avenue
Coronation party,
June 1953. At this time
rationing was still in force
for sugar, butter, cheese,
margarine and meat,
though sweets had been
taken off. A pint of milk
cost 2.5p, a bottle
of beer 4p and twenty
cigarettes 18p.

Smiling faces at the Town Hall during the Queen's silver jubilee visit to Grimsby in 1977. During her visit to the town Her Majesty opened a scented garden for the visually impaired in Haverstoe Park, Cleethorpes.

The tables were laid out, the kitchen chairs carried into the road, and pop bottles fizzed open. Councillor and Mrs Peter Willing, the Mayor and Mayoress of Grimsby, do their bit handing out the goodies at a local street party during the silver jubilee celebrations.

A nineteenth century view
of Victoria Street.

Carriers' carts in the Bull Ring 1908-10. The centre cart is advertising the then well
known Freshney's chemist shop next to the Black Swan in Victoria Street.

Victoria Street c1905 looking North East with the Black Swan on the left hand corner of the picture and Atkinson's Bon Ton shop on the right. Also advertised on the side of the building is Freshney's chemist.

The Black Swan on the corner of Victoria Street and Flottergate. This building was demolished in 1925 and a new pub with the same name was built in its place. The pub was finally demolished in 1971.

A few years later, about 1910, we're still on the Flottergate Victoria Street corner but looking towards the Corn Exchange.

The Palace Theatre and Palace Buffet, Victoria Street, in about 1906.

Victoria Street. There is a fair amount of traffic about but they are all
British-built. In fact between 1945 and 1950, the total number of cars
imported into the UK was just 3,749.

A view over the rooftops
looking down Victoria
Street South.

The Globe Cinema, Victoria Street, was, thanks to it having a few double seats, a favourite haunt of courting couples. However each of these seats had a slight ridge down the middle so as to create two seats in one. One of the films advertised on these pictures is Broadway, starring George Raft.

Victoria Street in August 1946, showing Pailthorp's Jewellers and the Post Office.

The old Royal National Mission to Deep Sea Fishermen, Riby Square.

Riby Square in about 1933, with the Sheffield Arms pictured on the left.

A trolleybus stands outside Whitehead's outfitters in Cleethorpe Road.
The No11 is en route for the Bathing Pool, Cleethorpes.

An aerial view taken from Riby Square looking down Freeman Street. In the foreground is Drakes furniture store but in the top right of the picture you can just see the Electric Power Station.

A trip to the seaside was only a bus ride away. Grimsby and Cleethorpes were unique in that though they were two separate towns, they operated a joint bus company. At peak times during the season there was a four-minute service on the No11 main route between the two towns.

Freeman Street Market.

'If it's raining or blowing a gale it must be market day'. According to stall holder Evelyn Nelson " On blowy days the wind whistled down the hill and the narrow streets and seemed to make a wind-tunnel that created a whirlwind on the market. The only thing to do then was to take down all the covers and let the wind blow through, or you had a sail and the stall and contents could easily blow over. It was terribly cold in winter. There were no lights unless you brought your own. It was a very healthy job though. I didn't have a cold for years." The stalls were erected on Thursdays and the stallholders arrived from 7.00am the following morning. White sheets were draped round the front of the stalls and linoleum cloths on the counters. Then came the goods. As the hygiene laws of the 30s, 40s, and 50s weren't as strict as they became in later years, some of the displays on the meat, fruit and farm produce stalls could on occasion be quite lavish. This picture was taken near Eason's corner.

This is Freeman Street in 1981. The absence of cars, buses, vans, lorries and the like was due to a pedestrian scheme that was being given a trial.

FREEMAN ST. MARKET

OPEN TUESDAY
FRIDAY
SATURDAY

OWNED & MANAGED BY
THE ENROLLED FREEMEN OF GRIMSBY
Tel. 56518 Market Superintendent R.T. CLIFFE.

GARIBALDI STREET

Joseph Samuel Bullen's photography shop at 183 Freeman Street in 1910.

The upstairs showroom of Gee's haberdashery and clothes shop in Freeman Street (above and right).

The queue outside the Regal cinema, Freeman Street. Built in 1937, the Regal – a
2,000-seat – super cinema, was officially opened by the mayor, Councillor
Charles E. Franklin. Those present were entertained by Wilfred Southworth playing
the mighty Crompton Organ – Here seems to have been a spot of rivalry between the
different cinema groups as to who could open the grandest cinema with the biggest,
bestest, loudest, organ – Wurlitzer or otherwise. The main feature on that opening
night was Fred Astaire and Ginger Rogers in the RKO picture Shall We Dance.

Freeman Street looking to the market and the ABC cinema.

The Old Market Place and
Corn Exchange. 1950.

The Old Market Place, date unknown, but probably post First World War.
There are plenty of hens and geese for sale.

The Old Market Place around 1900.

Waiting for a fare in the Old Market Place c1928. Freshney's later became Parker and Spyvee's.

Great Grimsby Street Tramways No39 stands outside St James' Church in 1928.

Cleethorpe Road level crossing, looking towards Riby Square. This crossing was the cause of major road congestion in Grimsby, and as we can see in this picture traffic is backed up beyond Riby Square. The only solution was to build a flyover.

A train heads out under the partially completed flyover.

Staff at the Premier Cinema pose for the camera in 1923. The current feature was Wembley – The World's Eighth Wonder. The top films of 1923 were Our Hospitality, which starred Buster Keaton, Natalie Talmadge, Joe Keaton and Buster Keaton Jnr, and Safety Last, the film that introduced cinema audiences to the hair-raising exploits of Harold Lloyd.

Chelmsford School with its open-air theatre can clearly be seen towards the top right of this picture taken in July 1962. Laceby Road runs across the picture from the bottom left hand corner. Winchester Avenue joins at the corner where St Mary's Church stands, while Worcester Avenue runs away in the opposite direction. Norwich Avenue, with the Oak Tree pub, is also well defined. Cambridge Road and Westward Ho stretch away towards the top of the photograph.

Shades of the country. A view of People's Park around 1910 taken from the Southworth Tower (named after the park's founder). The bandstand is pictured on the left, looking towards the pond and ice-cream parlour to the right.

This picture was taken at Nunsthorpe School in 1949 where the girls were having a Morris Dancing session.

The children of Victor Street, Guildford Street and Hilda
Street, smile for the cameraman on 21 August 1952.

The kids of Kent Street are in a party mood.
Coronation Day 1953.

The Tower Cinema, Kent Street, in March 1966.

Harold Wilson & Son butchers pictured on the corner of Chantry Lane.

A bird's eye view of Grimsby's biggest employer on the West Marsh. Peter Dixon's –
the enormous paper mill built on the former Gilbey Estates at Pyewipe, working at
full capacity when this picture was taken in February 1961.

A more industrial scene at the Electric Power Station, the cooling towers are distinctive on the skyline of several of the pictures throughout this chapter.

In 1805, the Haven Co, founded Grimsby's first dock (the New Dock) in the area currently known as the Riverhead. Prone to silting up, it was eventually relegated to being nothing more than a branch of the Royal Dock.

The paddle steamer Humber heads for Spurn with more than a full load of sightseers.

The Dock Tower is perhaps Grimsby's most famous landmark. The structure, which hides a 33,000-gallon capacity water tank, is based on a campanile in Sienna. Water from the tank allowed the lock gates to be opened hydraulically. Smaller water towers were built some years later and one of these can be seen at bottom right alongside the larger of the locks.

The Bury was one of five sisters built for the Great Central Railway for use on their lucrative North Sea routes. Launched in November 1910 and completed in 1911, Bury was usually to be found operating on the Grimsby – Hamburg service. During the war she and her surviving sisters (the Blackburn had sunk in 1910 following a collision off Sheringham) were converted into convoy rescue ships. This involved fitting her with extra accommodation, sick bay facilities, and additional life rafts. Based on the Clyde these ships accompanied convoys across the Atlantic saving hundreds of lives.

Completed in 1914, the Macclesfield was the last ship to be built for the Great Central Railway. She was placed on the Grimsby – Antwerp service while her sistership Chesterfield operated on the Grimsby – Rotterdam route. Chesterfield, requisitioned by the Admiralty in 1915, was torpedoed and sunk of Malta in 1918. Macclesfield survived both world wars.

The icehouse on the fish docks c1914.

Every year the Scottish herring fleet followed the fish around the coast. The catches were landed at the ports nearest the shoals so as not to lose valuable fishing time. At the ports the fishermen's wives, mothers, sisters, and aunts, prepared the herrings. As the fleet moved on, so did the women. This picture shows Scottish herring lasses at Grimsby during the 1907 season, packing the fish in salt.

Scottish lasses pack
herrings in barrels of salt
in Grimsby in 1914.

Henry (Harry) Carr fishcarter, with his rulley on the fish
docks 1907-08.

This atmospheric picture was taken at Alf Hunt Fish Merchants, Grimsby Fish Docks, in August 1903. Alf Hunt himself is in the picture – he's the one in the white hat. The company ceased trading in 1926.

This eight-stone cod was landed at Grimsby in 1929.

A pre-1910 view of the old fish Pontoon. One of the
boxes is stencilled T C Grey, they were a local fish
merchants based in Cleethorpes.

This picture of the outfitting jetties on the South Quay of No3 Fish Dock was taken in 1937. The jetty nearest the camera was 397ft long and equipped with a 5 ton travelling electric crane. The farther jetty, 266ft in length, had a travelling electric crane with a lift of 15 tons. A part of the North Wall can be seen in the distance along with the three coaling jetties.

This picture shows the wrecked bridge of the trawler Deerness which had been caught in the gale which accompanied the East Coast Floods of 1953.

Northern Foam high and dry on one of the slipways
situated along the South Quay of No3 Fish Dock.

This view of the Fish Docks
was taken in 1959 from
the dock tower. The old
Pontoon, where the fish
market now stands, can be
seen in the foreground.

Grimsby's famous North Wall. The funnel
markings of Diamonds Steam Fishing Co, Japan
Fishing Co, Onward Steam Fishing, and the Ross
Group are in evidence. The trawler nearest the
camera is the York City of Consolidated Fisheries.

This selection of pictures are a poignant reminder of the diversity of jobs and skills once required to make the docks run smoothly.

Standard Fishing Co.'s Sisapon was originally built for
the Royal Navy. She was one of the Military Class anti-
submarine trawlers ordered between 1942 and 1944
from Cooke, Welton & Gemmell, Beverley. Launched in
July 1944, she was commissioned into the Royal Navy as
HMT Royal Marine.

The former anti-submarine trawler HMT Pollock, seen here in her peacetime guise as Consolidated Fisheries' Swansea Castle.

Skipper Alf Walker of the Grimsby trawler Rose of England, gained a bit of a reputation for netting things other than fish. Back in 1952 a stone bowl came up during a haul in the North Sea and this wasn't Alf's first unusual object, he had already brought up some mammoth tusks. Alf's firm, Harry Franklin Ltd, decided to keep the bowl, but was anxious to find out what it was. The British Museum's Department of British and Medieval Antiquities, said that the bowl resembled a well known type of medieval mortar which was sometimes used as a holy water scoop.

The steam trawler Rodosto heads for the fishing grounds. Like so many other trawlers, Rodosto was requisitioned by the Admiralty in May 1915, remaining with the Royal Navy until returned to her owners in 1920.

Evening Telegraph photographer Dennis Arnold was sent on a trip to Iceland aboard the Consolidated Fisheries trawler Arsenal. We have included eight of the pictures he took.

Chief engineer Lenny Pye with the ship's cat.

The Arsenal's bridge.

Considered by many to be the most important man aboard – the cook.

Readying the trawl winch.

The busy scene on the Arsenal's fish pontoon. Crew members pictured here include:
John "Lofty" Walker, Ted Parmenter, Jack Scudder, George Farrow, Steve Brown and Geoff Carsberg.

Ted Parmenter, a colleague, and a respectable sized
halibut. On 23 October 1957, the Ross Group trawler
Stockham (skippered by Mr J Kerr), landed an 8ft long
halibut weighing 500lb (226.8 kilos), setting a post-war
record. And the price paid for it - £59 – was also
thought to be the record for a single fish at the time.
Bought by the Ross Group, who briefly used it for
publicity purposes.

A view from the starboard bridge wing.

The Northern Sceptre
looks very different in this
1956 picture. Icing-up is
dreaded of crews of ships
large and small alike.

Johnny Meadows proudly stands in front of the Ross Revenge, which he skippered on a number of record-breaking trips during the 1970s. In August 1976, she brought home 3,000 kits of fish worth £75,597 – a world record. Revenge was decommissioned from fishing and she would almost certainly have gone to the breakers had it not been for a group of men who had already turned British radio broadcasting on its head. They bought her to replace a leaky old tub called the Mi Amigo – better known as Radio Caroline – which had leaked a little too much and sunk. From 1983 until November 1990 Ross Revenge served as Radio Caroline.

It was on 25 April 1967 when news reached Grimsby that the trawler Brandur had been intercepted and arrested by the Icelandic gunboat Thor for allegedly fishing within the 12-mile limit. Four days later came news that had the whole town buzzing – the Brandur had done a runner. She had slipped out of Reykjavik under cover of darkness, passed two Icelandic gunboats without being challenged, and disappeared into the pitch black night. Skipper Bernard 'Bunny' Newton was making a dash for home, but what was even more astonishing was the fact that he had two Icelandic policemen "captive" on board. Gunboats gave chase – with orders to use force if necessary. After eleven hours the game was up, the Brandur, Newton and his crew were back in custody – they had managed to get 43 miles from Iceland.

Hauled before the court, Newton – who all along had protested his innocence- was found guilty of attempting to escape from arrest and obstructing the police, for which he was sentenced to three months. He was also fined 300,000 crowns – about £2,400 – for illegal fishing.

Cod Wars. Trawlers go about their business in the Icelandic fishing grounds while under Royal Navy protection.

Cod Wars. The Icelandic
gunboat Tyr attempts to
ram a Royal Navy warship
serving on Fishery
Protection Duties.

Cleethorpes

This aerial picture of Cleethorpes dates from about
1935. These days it is hard to imagine that on summer
Saturdays there could be between thirty and sixty
additional passenger trains using the station. Most of
these would be excursions bringing day-trippers.
The carriage sidings were more than adequate for
normal out of season traffic, but couldn't cope with such
large numbers of summer specials. Once the trains were
empty, they were shunted off to New Clee freight sidings

A step back in time to around 1910-11. Platform 6 is packed with trippers who have just detrained. Though there are attractions on the foreshore, we can see that this picture pre-dates the building of the fun fair.

The rain didn't stop the visitors from coming on Whit Monday 1954. Trains were still the main means of getting to the resort and the station would be the centre for much frenzied activity as eager and excited youngsters caught a glimpse of the beach. Many – and it is still true today – didn't venture much further than the "sands" opposite the bottom of the Station Approach. There were enough attractions nearby to keep them content until it was time to get the train home again.

The second of the new LNER locomotives to be named after famous football clubs, Grimsby Town ran her first journey on March 17, 1936 from Cleethorpes.

Britannia Class 4-6-2 No 70012 John of Gaunt on the turntable at Cleethorpes Station in 1965.

This fairly quiet view of Kingsway, looking south towards the bathing pool was taken around 1930.

This bustling view was taken from the pier in 1947, pictured on the far right is the Arcadia.

DANCING & ENTERTAINMENTS

MILK

Taken in 1937 this picture shows the pier intact.

During the 1920s one of the many attractions to be found at Wonderland was the Mancho Tables.

The Big Dipper at Wonderland. It was finally demolished in 1974.

Some things never change. People still enjoy getting their shoes and socks off and dipping their toes in the tide.

Edwardian elegance comes to Cleethorpes.

A step back in time to those sunny summer days between the wars. The girls from Gee's haberdashery and clothes shop, Freeman Street, on one of their regular Thursday afternoon trips to Cleethorpes.

This picture of Cleethorpes boating lake was taken in 1930, only a year after it had been completed.

Coastal erosion at Sea Bank Road (now a part of Kingsway), in 1902, caused by the soft boulder clay being washed away. At the beginning of the twentieth century a surprising number of resorts had houses like these; built close to the sea with little thought of protection.

The bottom picture was taken in the aftermath of the East Coast Floods of 1953 and shows the devastating effect of wind and wave action on the railway line at Cleethorpes – the trackbed has been completely washed away. The flooding affected 1,500 homes in the town and damage ran into millions of pounds.

This picture taken in 1928 is of the first pupils to attend the newly opened Reynolds Street School, Cleethorpes. The headmaster is Mr England, and the teacher is Miss Davies.

VE Day celebrations, George Street, Cleethorpes.

Celebrations of a different kind. It is 1977 and the children of Woodsley Avenue
celebrate the Queen's silver jubilee.

An aerial view of Blundell
Park taken about 1946-47.

Out and About

Our first view in this chapter is of St Peter's Church in
Humberston. The tower of the church dates from the

A picturesque view of Brigsley.

A walk down the lane
in Beelsby.

In the background a wagon loaded high with sacks of potatoes heads for Ludborough station as workmen carry out improvements to Fulstow crossroads. The picture was taken around 1920-21 and the workmen appear to be removing an island from the junction. The Cross Keys pub would be just off the picture on the right hand side.

This picture was taken in the yard at Sea Farm, Grainthorpe, probably during the First World War.

Charlie Parker enjoys a "cuppa" and Charlie Jacklin keeps his eye on the traction engine controls as it powers a threshing machine. Propping up the front wheel of the engine is farmer William Stones – his lads Fred and Alfred are by the rear wheel.

On the last day of January 1953 much of the East Coast of England was devastated by a storm surge, as a 90mph north westerly gale whipped up sea levels to nearly three metres above normal high water levels, causing huge waves to smash through, or pour over coastal defences. In this picture people are being evacuated from Mablethorpe. Every available means of transport was pressed into service including this farm tractor and trailer. This picture was first published on 2 February 1953.

East Coast Floods of 1953.
This is the High Street,
Mablethorpe.

Come number 5, yer time's up! An abandoned boat drifts
along Mablethorpe High Street.

Members of the Salvation Army arrive in Mablethorpe with a lorry load of supplies.

East Coast Floods of 1953. Sutton-on-Sea railway station flooded out. Further south the flood defences at Boston were breached and homes flooded. At Wisbech over 1,000 homes had to be evacuated and at Hunstanton hundreds of caravans were swept away. Canvey Island suffered most. Here every home had to be evacuated, as the flood defences were totally overwhelmed, leaving the whole island underwater

This peaceful scene from the 1950s is of the lake in Tathwell.

Making a splash through
the brook at Cawthorpe.

St Mary's church in Ludborough.

A view of the wolds taken from Cawkwell Hill.
Labouring up the hill is the No 14 bus to Louth.

The Kings Head in Tealby is said to date back to the 14th Century.

A quiet road in Kelsey.

One of George Johnson's Bedford cattle trucks at the petrol pump in North Kelsey High Street. By 1947 George's fleet included: four Bedford cattle vans, two Bedford tippers, two Commers and a Vulcan. The Primitive Methodist Chapel no longer stands. It was bought by George and demolished to make way for a bungalow. Petrol rationing remained in force throughout the 1940s and in 1948 the government ordered that fuel used in commercial vehicles, tractors, and so on should be dyed red.

George Johnson and his brother Arthur deliver coal around North Kelsey with the aid of a Bedford two tonner.

George's two tonners were kept busy at hay making time.

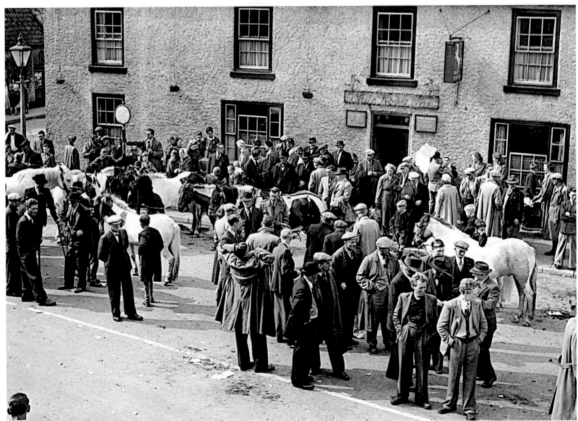

The fortunes of the annual Brigg Horse Fair have fluctuated tremendously since the end of the Second World War. This picture was taken in 1955 when the event was still held in the street - a sight once common throughout the country. The White Horse – still a popular Brigg hostelry – would have done a roaring trade once the buying and selling was over.

Moving forward in time to the Brigg Horse Fair of 1977. Among the spectators was
Councillor Terry Atherton (left), from Kirton, who was later to become the first leader
of Glanford Borough Council. With him, and enjoying a novel taste of British heritage,
were civic visitors from Culemborg in the Netherlands.

St Bartholomew's church
in Keelby.

There is not much traffic on the road going through Keelby village.

Crowds gather near the double-ended paddle steamer
Killingholme during the official opening of Immingham Dock
by King George V and Queen Mary on 22 July 1912.

On the outbreak of the Great War the Admiralty wasted little time in utilising Immingham Docks as a base for minesweepers and auxiliary patrol vessels. This picture, taken on the mineral quay, shows women splicing ropes for minesweeper paravanes.

Immingham Docks in the 1950s.

One of the original Great Central Railway trams arrives from Grimsby at the
Immingham Town stop in Queen's Road on 22 July 1956. Increased passenger figures
and the need to replace some of the more decrepit rolling stock saw the purchase in
1951 of no less than 19 trams from the Gateshead and District Tramways Co.
However by the late-50s the service had been reduced to peak times only, the line
closing altogether in July 1961.

Early spring flowers from the nurseries of A R and V Johnson at Cottagers' Plot,
Laceby. The picture was taken in January 1953 among the ladies with the flowers
are: Mrs Kathleen Johnson, Mrs Violet Altoft, Miss Vera Johnson, and
Mrs Margaret Millgate.

A quiet country lane with Stallingborough Mill on the right. The windmill sails look to be in need of some repair in this picture.

Stallingborough Grange is pictured here with the mill in the background.

Sport & Leisure

Grimsby Town FC line-up for the 1929-30 season.
Back row: Jock Priestley, Jack Prior, Charlie Wilson,
Tommy Read, Arthur Bateman, Herbert Woods (trainer)
and Teddy Buck. Front row: Tim Coleman, Jackie Bestall,
Joe Robson, Steve Coglin, Billy Marshall and Charlie Wrack.

Ernest "Tim" Coleman made 87 league appearances for Grimsby Town between 1929 and 1933 during which he scored 57 goals.

Grimsby Town FC in the 1930s. Among those pictured are Harry Betmead (back extreme left), George Tweedy (back, fourth from left), Jackie Bestall (front, third left) and Pat Glover (front, fourth from left). Glover signed for the Mariners in December 1928. After initially struggling to secure a first team spot, he came into his own in the 1933-34 season. For the next four seasons he scored 42, 34, 31 and 29 goals in the league. During his stay at Grimsby, Glover was also selected to play for Wales. At the end of the 1939 season he moved to Plymouth Argyle, a move that some believe robbed Grimsby of one of its greatest ever players.

Pat Glover quit football at the end of the war to become licensee of the King's Arms in Tamerton Foliot, a village near Plympton, Devon. Our picture was taken some years later when three Grimsby friends, Vernon Godwin, Geoff Fox and Wally Hanson, set off on a motorcycle tour around Devon. Stopping off at the King's Arms for a swift one, they were amazed to find it was non other than Pat serving up the stuff of life. In this picture Pat is at second right.

Without doubt Billy Cairns was one of the game's greatest headers of the ball. He said "Heading is a soccer art, and as such should be studied extensively. It develops and co-ordinates the senses of mind and eye...Head and ball should connect when the player is at the peak of his spring."

Grimsby Town arrive home at the station triumphant after winning promotion to Division Two by beating Brentford 2-0 in the final game with goals from Ron Rafferty and Cliff Portwood. Captain Keith Jobling is held aloft by Brian Keeble (left) and Tony Knights.

The Grimsby Town squad in the summer of 1972, preparing for their first season back in Division Three. Back row left to right: Stuart Gray, Mike Hickman, Dave Booth, Clive Wigginton, Harry Wainman, Lew Chatterley, Matt Tees, Graham Rathbone, Barry Lynch. Front Row from the left: Dave Boylen, Paddy Campbell, Dave Worthington, Lawrie McMenemy (manager), Jack Lewis, Allan Gauden, Stuart Brace.

Former England manager Graham Taylor during his playing days at Grimsby Town.

Mike Hickman in action at Blundell Park during the 1971-72 season. Although not the most gifted of forwards, Mike was a big-hearted player whose hard-working style endeared him to the fans. He also scored a good number of goals. The Grimsby player on the left is Stuart Brace whose pace and finishing ability made him one of the most prolific post-war marksmen at Blundell Park. On the extreme right is David Boylen, midfield architect of the side when Laurie McMenemy was manager.

Legendary striker Matt Tees, in action during Grimsby Town's division four championship winning season of 1971-72. The veteran's goals played a vital part in the Mariners climbing out of the basement section of the Football League but injuries were beginning to take their toll on Matt's wiry frame and he retired the following season. He is one of Grimsby Town's most popular players of all time.

Pick that one out! One of Alan Gauden's pair in the home match against Peterborough in that famous 1971-72 season.

Striker Jimmy Lumby signed full-time for Grimsby Town in 1973.

Joe Waters, Grimsby Town skipper in the 1980s.

A sport of a different kind brought spectators flocking to Blundell Park back in June 1924 – a motor cycle football match.

Grimsby Town Boys team
on 13 September 1952.
Back row: Tom Parkinson,
Oscar Slosmanis, Terry
Parker, Doug Marsh,
Dorphin, Ted Nicholson.
Front row: Bracey,
Peter Lavevick, Bridges,
Brickley and Ward.

Macaulay Street School football team 1919-20 season. The teacher is Mr F. A. Foster.
The boys are, back row: S Marshall, A Monk, A Jones, J Riley. The two boys kneeling
are Alec Wood and S Ellis. Front row: F Walmsley, R Clark, H Bell, S Pullen and
C Cooling. Note the clock. These seemed to be popular trophies at that time.

Nunsthorpe School football team 1949-50 season. The school strip comprised a mixture of collared and v-neck quartered pattern wool shirts, hooped socks and an interesting assortment of shorts. It looks as though shin pads are just catching on. At some schools the boys often bought pads themselves as they were not a part of the school kit.

Freddie Frith waves goodbye to his wife as he leaves home to ride in the 1949 TT races on the Isle of Man.

The Grimsby Harriers show off some of their trophies and individual medals in this picture from the early-30s.
The club had taken Lincolnshire cross-country championship in 1911, 1912, 1914, 1920 and 1931. They had been
Hull & District cross-country champions for three years in a row – 1927 to 1929. Similarly, they had taken the
Hull & district junior cross-country championship for four years on the trot – 1925 to 1928. If that wasn't enough,
they also dominated the Beverley & District championships, lifting the cross-country title in 1927, 1928, and 1929,
and the junior title from 1925, to 1928. In 1928 they also won the Radiance Challenge Cup.

Members of the Brigg
Small Bore Rifle Club in
the mid-30s. Holding the
trophy is David Briggs, at
the time senior partner in
estate agents and auctioneers
Briggs and Holmes.

The Grimsby Ladies Rifle Club were formidable opponents, winning county league competitions that included men's teams.

Victoria Street School swimming team, 1923.

HOT
BATHS
ANY PERSON
TO THE
BATHS SUPT
DEEP END
4FT 6IN
NO SMOKING

It looks like these lads are enjoying themselves at the local swimming baths.

BATHERS MUST VACATE THE BATH 15 MINUTES BEFORE SESSION ENDS SO AS TO LEAVE THE BUILDING AT THE END OF THE ALLOTTED PERIOD
4FT 6IN

The ladies of the Cleethorpes Rink Hockey Club 1910-11.

The Grimsby and
Cleethorpes School of
Physical Culture.

When the Channel Fleet paid a visit to Grimsby in 1907 organisers arranged for several sporting events. Games of cricket and athletics were played and finally a game of tug of war.

Linked together as they skate round the old
Grimsby ice rink on Ladysmith Road.

Ray Edmonds pictured
here in 1969 holding his
trophy for the English
amateur snooker
championship.

When Duty Calls

This picture, taken at the Riby Square end of Freeman
Street in 1915, shows the funeral parade for members of
the crew of HM submarine E13, killed in action on
19 August. The submarine had run aground in

The paddle steamer
Cleethorpes saw service
with the Royal Navy
during the Great War as
an auxiliary minesweeper.

Northern Gem when serving with the Royal Navy during the Second World War.

On the morning of
31 October 1943, a motor
gunboat – the Gay Viking
– docked at Immingham.
She was one of five MGBs
allocated by the Admiralty
to run between the
Humber and the Swedish
port of Lysekil, where they
would load and bring back
machine tools, ball
bearings, components, and
other materials essential
to the war-effort.
Each boat was provided
with a defensive armament
comprising 20mm
Oerlikons and machine guns.

HMS Ariadne docks at Grimsby in October 1979 for an official visit to Scunthorpe, the town having adopted the frigate in 1973. Ariadne was the last of the Leander Class frigates to enter service.

The pavements are packed with onlookers and local residents take advantage of the views from their bedroom windows as Grimsby celebrates the coronation of King George V. Nearest the camera are members of D Squadron, the Lincolnshire Yeomanry (The Chums). 23 June 1911.

Soldiers, including a Grimsby Chum (extreme right) on a machine gun training course at Strensall Barracks, York, in 1915.

During the Second World War the Haile and Bull Sands forts were home to the batteries of the 513th Coast Regiment.

This picture of members of 384 Coy, 46th AA Battalion, was taken at a TA annual camp at Burnham Beeches, between Barton and Brigg in August 1939.

Members of the Scunthorpe 384 Coy on exercise with a tripod-mounted Lewis gun in August 1939.

Members of 384 Coy with a sound locator. Though we would consider this piece of kit to be somewhat primitive, it was capable of picking up the sounds made by the unsynchronised engines of approaching German aircraft.

Grub's up! Troops on anti-invasion duty in the summer of 1940.

Home Guardsmen attend a demonstration firing of a
Northover Projector.

No2 platoon of A Company, of the Conisholme and Grainthorpe Home Guard in 1941.
By May 1941 some 1.6 million men had volunteered for the Home Guard, and, more
importantly, they were becoming better trained and better armed. Gradually ever more
sophisticated weaponry became available, such as Browning Automatic Rifles and sten guns.

A rather worn, but nevertheless historically important local picture. Taken at Cherry Garth, Humberston, possibly in 1942/43, it shows members of B Company, 5th Lindsey Battalion, Home Guard. Ron Thompson, who served in the Humberston Home Guard, was convinced that his unit compared very well with the BBC comedy series Dad's Army.

As the winter of 1940 took hold, there was a massive drive throughout the country to provide comforts for the troops of the British Expeditionary Force stationed in France. At local cinemas there were scenes such as this one as ladies, armed with needles and wool got together for some serious knitting. Some voluntary groups assembled individual parcels - each containing cigarettes, chocolate, soap, biscuits, socks, a scarf, perhaps a magazine or two. These were sent to the BEF where they were distributed one to each soldier.

The East Coast Floods 1953. This picture was published on 14 February 1953 and shows the Duchess of Gloucester inspecting the temporary sea defences being thrown up around Mablethorpe by troops.

The East Coast Floods 1953. Harold Macmillan, then Minister of Health, toured the devastated areas. He is seen here holding a press-call at RAF Manby. Grimsby Evening Telegraph reporter Eric Sheckell is second from the left.

The East Coast Floods 1953. The RAF lends a hand at
evacuating the residents of Mablethorpe.

Another scene from Maplethorpe of the East Coast Floods of 1953 shows an army lorry that was being used for rescue work, turned on its side in a ditch.

A royal visit in 1958 as the Queen inspects an RAF guard of honour.

A Lincoln bomber flies over Grimsby in May 1949.

Lightning interceptor attack aircraft line up on the
runway at RAF Binbrook at the 25th anniversary of the
aircrafts introduction to the RAF.

A No11 Squadron Mk6 Lightning lands at RAF Binbrook in March 1972.
The Mk6 was the full production version of the Mk3A, its over-wing tanks nearly
doubling the aircraft's fuel capacity.

Lightnings fly in formation
above RAF Binbrook
during the base's last Open
Day on 22 August 1987.
No5 Squadron converted
to the Tornado and moved
to RAF Coningsby and
No11 Squadron was
moved to RAF Leeming.

The rain soaked scene at RAF Binbrook during the base's last Open Day.

Preparing for all eventualities. A firefighting exercise at Binbrook.

Not long after it had closed RAF Binbrook was alive once more with the sound of aircraft, albeit for just a few short weeks. The airfield had been chosen for location filming for the movie Memphis Belle, the story of a B17 Flying Fortress. Our picture shows three of the five B17's that were brought together for the film. Binbrook had a similar layout to the original Memphis Belle's base at Brassingbourne in Cambridgeshire. Some alterations to Binbrook were carried out including the removal of the ASP lighting system, the disguising of modern buildings, and the construction of a World War Two type control tower. Many Grimsby locals answered the ad in the Evening Telegraph to work as extras.

During World War II the operational life expectancy for the Lancaster bomber was estimated to be just 40 hours. Little wonder then that during the summer of 1944 the rivalry between the resident squadrons at RAF Skellingthorpe was soaring to an all time high. No's 50 and 61squadrons each had a Lancaster nearing its 'century' – a hundred operations. No 50 Squadron got there first when Lancaster ED588 VN-G – better known as 'N-Nan' safely returned from a raid over Vitry-la-Francois on 28 June. No61 Squadron's 'G-George' completed her century on 4 July.